THE VW BEETLE

A CELEBRATION OF THE VW BUG

THE VW BEETLE

A CELEBRATION OF THE VW BUG

Cabriolet

CHRISTY CAMPBELL

HAMLYN

Published in 1990
by The Hamlyn Publishing Group Limited
a division of The Octopus Publishing Group,
Michelin House, 81 Fulham Road, London SW3 6RB

ISBN 0 600 56814 8

Produced by Mandarin Offset
Printed in Hong Kong

Half-title page: *Flower power Beetle.*
Title page: *On the left are pages from the original brochure for the KdF-Wagen which includes the order form. On the right is another picture from a brochure, this time of the Karmann Ghia cabriolet.*

ACKNOWLEDGEMENTS

The publishers would like to thank the following organisations and individuals for their kind permission to reproduce the photographs in this book:

Fotohaus Keiper: 74-75
Foto Strenger GMBH: 72
Haymarket Motoring Archives: 40-41, 73, 78-79
David Hodges Collection: 2
The International Vintage Volkswagen Magazine/Bob Shail: 11 top, 15, 16 top, 18-19, 21, 22 top left, 22 bottom left, 22-23, 24 top, 25 top, 30 bottom, 37 bottom, 37 top, 42-43
Leigh Jones Collection: 36 top
Mike Key: 45 bottom, 52, 53, 58-59, 62 top right, 65 left, 66, 68-69, 69 top, 70-71

Andrew Morland: 26, 34 top, 63 top, 62-63, 64-65, 76-77
The National Motor Museum, Beaulieu: 9 top and bottom, 10, 11 bottom, 12 top, 12-13, 13 top, 16-17, 28-9, 29 bottom, 31 bottom, 32 top, 33 bottom, 44, 46 bottom, 49 bottom, 50-1, 51, 54, 55, 56 top left, 56 top centre, 56-7, 57 top left, 66-7,/Nicky Wright 46 top
Quadrant: 6, 7, 8, 14 top, 16 bottom, 28 bottom, 41, 45 top, 47 top, 48 top and bottom, 79 top
Terry Schuler/Club of America Vintage Volkswagen: 27, 30 top, 32 bottom, 33 top, 36 bottom, 40, 43, 50 top, 60-61, 62 top left
Octopus Group Ltd.,: 38, Jasper Spencer Smith 31 top
Volkswagen: 1, 3, 14-15, 18, 24-25, 47 bottom
Zefa Picture Library: 34 bottom, 35, 39, 42 (inset), 49 top

CONTENTS

CHAPTER ONE

SOMETHING NAZI IN THE WOODSHED

LEGEND MIGHT HAVE IT THAT THE VOLKSWAGEN WAS THE

CREATION OF ONE MAN, DR FERDINAND PORSCHE, WHO

VIRTUALLY BUILT THE FIRST VW FROM SCRATCH. BUT THIS MOST

SIGNIFICANT MOTOR CAR DREW ON A RICH CLIMATE OF

EUROPEAN ENGINEERING INNOVATION, AND IT WAS BACKED

BY THE RESOURCES OF RUTHLESS STATE POWER.

Above: *Dr Ferdinand Porsche (far left) points out the details of the KdF Wagen to his Führer.*
Left: *One of the batch of 44 VW38 pre-production prototypes built in 1938.*

It was a Nazi state occasion and the cameras of the Reich's propaganda ministry were there to record everything in glorious colour. Huge swastika banners fluttered in the spring breeze. Hitler Youth drummers beat out a solemn tattoo, increasing the tension as 70,000 spectators waited for the Führer to arrive. He would preside at the ceremonial laying of the foundation stone for a new factory. Carved deep into its face was the swastika-in-a-cogwheel symbol of the German Labour Front (DAF).

Uniformed Nazi dignatories beamed as Hitler inspected models of the product the factory would make. Among the brown and gold uniforms of the DAF and the black and silver of the SS, there was a figure in a rumpled civilian suit. Hitler described him as 'Germany's greatest automobile engineer.' His name was Ferdinand Porsche.

This day, 26 May 1938, marked the inception of KdF-Stadt, 'Strength Through Joy City.' The factory, next to a showpiece worker's town near Hanover, would produce Hitler's promised 'People's Car.' Porsche, the chief designer, was proud and relieved, as a column of prototype Volkswagens arrived at the base of the podium to take dignatories on test runs. Hitler (who could not drive) eased himself into a cabriolet version, Porsche at his side. The Führer was pleased.

After more than half a century, it still comes as a stark surprise to see the pictures of the KdF-Stadt ceremony. It is like seeing Hitler taking a swig from a Coke bottle or clutching a Filofax. That little hump-backed motor car endured and prospered, becoming a symbol of automotive reason in an age of conspicuous consumption. Hitler's demented dreams of world conquest died with him in his Berlin bunker. It was Volkswagen which would conquer the world.

The 'Beetle' is the most popular car in history. Its success played no small part in the rebuilding of the country on which Hitler had brought down such terrible devastation. Its engineering formula (especially its rear-mounted, air-cooled engine) may eventually have proved a blind-alley for Volkswagen, but its practicality, ease of maintenance and build-quality will ensure that the Beetle's shape (and its sound) will stay with us for another 50 years or more.

How the Beetle conquered the world has a lot to do with the genius of the company's post-war management. But without Porsche's basic product, noisy, unorthodox, and to many eyes, ugly, there would have been nothing.

To understand such a phenomenon it is necessary to understand the climate in which it was conceived.

Ferdinand Porsche, born in Bohemia in 1875, had built his first car for the Viennese coachbuilder, Ludwig Lohner, in 1900. As a young journeyman, he moved on to Austro-Daimler, then to the original German Daimler company in 1923 as technical director. When Daimler merged with Benz to form Daimler-Benz in 1926, he designed the formidable 7.1-litre SS and SSK Sports cars before falling out spectacularly with the management when they blocked his plans for a small car called the Type 130.

So he returned to Austria in 1928 to work for the Steyr company where he designed the 5.3-litre straight-eight 'Austria' with independent rear springing by swing axles. As the Wall Street crash and its fallout rocked Steyr, Porsche took the bold step of setting up his own automotive design business.

It would be a consultancy, formed from a nucleus of talented engineers and aerodynamicists, based in Stuttgart, the heart of the German motor industry. From Steyr, Porsche took Josef Kales,

Adolf Hitler presides over the KdF-Stadt factory foundation stone-laying ceremony on 26 May 1938 with saloon and cabriolet VW38 prototypes on hand to led crediibility to what was still at this stage a 'paper' car.

Porsche showed his flair for sporting cars early. The Austro-Daimler 'Sascha' won its class in the 1922 Targa Florio race.

an aero-engine designer, and Karl Frölich, a gearbox specialist. An old associate, Karl Rabe, was lured from Austro-Daimler as chief engineer with Josef Mickl, aerodynamics expert. Porsche's 20-year-old son, Ferry, was also put to work.

Two months before Porsche's design office opened in December 1930, Hitler's National Socialist Workers Party had become the second largest party in Germany's parliament, the Reichstag.

Porsche was to play a significant part in its destiny, although he did not know it yet. At first there was only a trickle of work, but enough to attract new talent, including a 27-year-old body-designer called Erwin Komenda.

One of his first tasks was a large luxury car for Wanderer which was significant in that it featured integral headlamps in the front wings and a long curved rear-end like the Beetle-to-be.

At the same time, Porsche was shrewd enough to undertake an in-house project for a small, cheap and hopefully affordable car – his design Type 12. Once again, Komenda did the styling and the result was like the larger Wanderer.

The motorcycle firm Zündapp decided at this time to get into the small car market, and commissioned an exotic prototype with rear-mounted engine, central backbone chassis, all round independent suspension and an alligator front lid closing on the luggage space and spare wheel. The whole thing looked very Beetle-like. Three prototypes were assembled in 1932, but the project remained stillborn. Porsche received 85,000 Marks for his work and kept the design.

A decade later Porsche's thoughts were turning to advanced engineering for everyman. The prototype Type 32 built for NSU in 1934 had a backbone chassis and rear-mounted, air-cooled engine.

The concept went further with another motorcycle maker, NSU. This would be Porsche's Type 32, with torsion bar suspension and an air-cooled front four-cylinder engine. Three prototype Type 32s were built before NSU baulked at the investment required to productionize the vehicle.

Then, in January 1933 Hitler came to power on a promise to bring order, full employment and military greatness to Germany.

The revival of military strength would first demand economic revival – and the creation of an industrial base with the trained manpower and the capital equipment to turn out mass-produced motor vehicles, tanks and aircraft.

Stage one of Hitler's plan was a network of motorways to soak up unemployment. These new superhighways were, according to Hitler's propaganda, escape-lanes for the German masses seeking rewards for their labours in the form of radio sets and automobiles through the Nazi leisure organisation *Kraft durch Freude* (Strength Through Joy).

'Why should millions of good, hard-working people not own motor cars?' asked Hitler at the opening of the 1934 Berlin Motor Show, a year after his seizure of power. The idea of a Volkswagen, the 'people's car', had been current in Germany since the mid 1920s when Hitler wrote his autobiography and political testament *Mein Kampf*. One of his political disciples was a fellow Austrian, a manager at Daimler-Benz named Jakob Werlin. Hitler was fascinated by motor cars, and used them (and later aircraft and radio) to span distances like no politician before.

Ten years on, with Hitler now Reichschancellor, Werlin was the intermediary between Hitler and Porsche, summoning the designer to a meeting at the Kaiserhof Hotel in Berlin. The meeting, in May 1934, was short and to the point. Hitler outlined what he wanted, a car for the people – which could accommodate two adults and three children and propel them at 100 kmh (62 mph) at a fuel consumption of 6 litres per 100 km (33 mpg). The Führer – leader – had some pronounced ideas on the basic engineering, insisting that the car should be air-cooled and cost only 1,000 Reichsmarks (about £86).

Porsche's work on the Zündapp and NSU prototypes had illustrated the problems of making this kind of engineering work

cheaply. But they formed the basis on his new people's car.

The 'streamlined' shape was critical. Streamlining was the magical marketing word of the Thirties, as 'atomic' was to the Fifties, a symbol of modernity and dynamism. Hitler and the National Socialists saw the efficiency of form and function in engineering as fundamental, whether the product was to be a machine-pistol, a fighter aircraft, or a people's car.

In Germany, the science of automobile aerodynamics had been elevated to the highest plane with large scale state investment in research and wind-tunnel facilities.

The two men who led the way were both born in Vienna: Edmund Rumpler and Paul Jaray. Rumpler was a motor engineer who discovered aircraft, then returned to automobiles. In 1902 at the age of thirty he had been appointed technical director of Adler. A year later he filed a basic patent for a live swing axle, allowing the independent suspension of driving wheels. In 1908 he formed Rumpler aircraft works, going on to design and build a range of significant aircraft for the Imperial German air force. That all ended with the German defeat – and Rumpler departed the turmoil of revolutionary Berlin for Bavaria to play once again with motor-cars.

His Tropfen-Wagen appeared in 1921 featuring a rear mounted engine in a befinned, 'teardrop' shaped body, developed with the aid of a wind-tunnel. But it was too far ahead of its time and sales were low.

Paul Jaray had worked on airship design for the German Navy. Like Rumpler, he turned to automotive design after the war, filing a series of patents for aerodynamically efficient car body design (and encountering a series of legal clashes with Rumpler as a result). Jaray was a purist who paid little regard to the pleadings of marketing men or even mechanical engineers to deviate just a little from his basic concept. In the late 1920s and early 1930s his 'perfect' body form with a long sloping rear was applied to a number of chassis from German firms.

As it happened his shape was imperfect, but a modified version appeared on a luxurious, aerodynamically advanced saloon – the Tatra Type 87, made in Czechoslovakia. Like the Beetle, it incorporated an air-cooled, rear-mounted engine and a backbone chassis. It was the work of one of Europe's most significant automotive designers, Hans Ledwinka.

The Case of the Squashed Bug

The story of Ledwinka, born at Klosterneuberg near Vienna on 4 February 1878, touches more than once on the Beetle saga. Born three years after Porsche, and a fellow subject of the Habsburgs, Ledwinka had first become involved with the construction of automobiles in 1897 at Nesseldorf Imperial and Royal Carriage Factory. His career progressed in a shower of inventiveness, taking him eventually to Steyr, where he designed both innovative luxury cars and heavy trucks. But Steyr could not afford to put his concepts for small cars into production.

Over the border in the new state of Czechoslovakia, however, the Ringhoffer company was prepared to offer the celebrated designer his chance. The results would be significant.

Ledwinka took with him the plans for a cheap and rugged vehicle with a central tube backbone chassis, powered by a front-mounted horizontally-opposed two-cylinder engine using forced air-cooling, the flywheel doubling as a fan. It was to be the first product of the Ringhoffer-Tatra motor works (newly named after

Streamline pioneer Edmund Rumpler's *Tropfen-wagen* of 1921, designed with the aid of a wind tunnel, was a landmark in automobile aerodynamics, but was too far ahead of its time for sales success.

Hans Ledwinka's work for the Czech firm of Tatra produced one of the century's most significant cars. The Type 77 (**above**) of 1934 featured a backbone chassis, with a 3.4-litre air-cooled V8 mounted behind the rear axles. The Type 87 of 1937 (**below**) refined the concept with a lighter, 2.9-litre engine and a claimed top speed of 95mph.

Far Left: Hans Ledwinka, the Austrian-born automotive genius who paralleled Porsche in many of the technical innovations that led to the VW. **Above:** The Tatra Type 97, the rival bug, squashed when Czechoslovakia was occupied by the Germans. **Below:** The Tatra Type 77a of 1936 combined elegance and aerodynamic efficiency — and coefficient of drag was 0.212.

the nearby mountain range) at Koprivinice in eastern Moravia.

Hitler used one extensively for his rabble-rousing tours of Germany in the early 1920s and some were still running as daily transport 40 years later. Most popular of all was the Type 57 built from 1930 onwards (and under license in Germany) with a four-cylinder 1,160cc engine.

By the late 1920s Ledwinka was exploring the prospect of mounting his proven, but noisy, air-cooled engine at the rear of a new design. Rear engines meant that (for the driver at least) the noise would be left behind and the layout fitted in with the 'new' automotive concept of streamlining.

The Tatra Type 570 prototype of 1933 carried its air-cooled 850cc twin-cylinder engine in its tail, mounted on the end of the chassis tube, wrapped in a Beetle-like body with long sloping louvred back with a front end featuring a pronounced rounded prow and frogeye headlights.

Later Porsche, in his own words, admitted that he occasionally 'looked over the shoulder' of his great contemporary. As Ledwinka produced some great luxury cars, he worked on smaller versions, including the Type 97 with a rear-mounted 1,761cc air-cooled engine. The body was very Beetle like, with a fastback louvred tail – and no rear window. When the Type 97 appeared in

Above and below: A cabriolet version of the VW was envisaged right from the beginning of the project but although the joys of an open People's Car featured in early KdF publicity, only one hand-built prototype was produced. **Far right:** VW3 series prototype of 1936 shows oval engine-louvring and absence of rear windows.

1938 it was perhaps the most advanced small car in the world. But it was expensive – listed at more than five and a half times the KdF-Wagen's target selling price. Like the Czech Republic, its days were numbered. In two bites Nazi Germany gobbled up the independent state in 1938 and 1939 turning it into a 'protectorate' of the Reich. The Tatrawerke was now just an adjunct of the German armaments industry and the Type 97 line was shut down after only 500 had been built. Ten legal claims by Tatra against VW for infringement of patents went the same way in the face of Nazi *force majeure* – although after the war the case was re-opened and rumbled on for years. In 1961, Volkswagen eventually made a settlement, but Ledwinka never received any money. He died in relative obscurity in 1967.

Porsche, like Ledwinka, had a bank of work on which to draw. The idea of a central backbone had been explored by Rover in 1904, the French firm of Simplicia in 1909, then by Tatra. In 1926 a Vienna-born engineering student named Béla Barényi completed his thesis on the design of a radically new motor-car featuring a central tube frame and a flat four, air-cooled, rear-mounted engine, the whole thing apart from its leaf springs, strikingly like a Beetle. Barényi claimed to have shown his plans to Porsche in 1931.

Whatever claims may have been made later, Porsche had the talented engineers around him, the experience of advanced chassis design, and the unique authority of the Führer's will to make the whole thing happen.

His Büro began serious design studies in April 1934, using the rear-engined, streamlined Type 32 as a starting point. Hitler saw the plans for the 'Type 60' a month later, insisting on a lower bonnet line and emphasising in particular the importance of good streamlining.

On 22 June 1934, Porsche signed a detailed contract with the German automotive industry association (the Reichsverbandes der Deutschen Automobil-Industrie or RDA) for development of the project with a down payment of £20,000 to produce the proto-types within 10 months.

It was an impossible deadline. Porsche's operation was too small. The 'sponsoring' organisation, the RDA, which represented the giants of German automotive industry, was far from enthusiastic. It was being told to underwrite a venture that, if it succeeded, would attack the profits of its member companies. But when Porsche failed to meet the delivery target, government pressure was applied even more strongly on all parties.

Over the winter of 1934-5, two Type 60 vehicles (V1 and V2 – from the German *Versuchs* – experimental), were put together in the spacious garage of Porsche's Stuttgart home. They had bodywork built by Reutter (V1, the saloon) and Drauz (V2, a cabriolet). They were certainly Beetle-like, with flowing curves and Hitler's low-bonnet line. Headlights were mounted frogeye style at the front of the bonnet. Doors were forward opening, there was no rear window, and the engine cover has prominent louvres. Under the skin, the backbone chassis layout of the Type 32 was refined with an arched cross section and integral cross-members front and rear. Suspension was again by torsion bar all round. The frame was forked at its rear-end to take the engine and gearbox.

Experimental two-cylinder and four-cylinder, two-stroke, engines were tried and rejected. The V1 had a two-cylinder, air-

The V1/V2 chassis, completed in late 1935 with torsion-bar suspension, acted as testbeds for several engine configurations including two- and four-stroke two-cylinder and four-cylinder horizontally-opposed 'boxermotors'. The two-cylinder boxer 'D-Motor' shown here was unacceptably noisy and underpowered.

The VW's air-cooled engine, with its horizontally opposed pistons, was a triumph of simplicity. But there was a five year period of development and several false-starts before the definitive 'E-Motor' (**above**) emerged to power the KdF-Wagen. **Right:** The VW30 of 1937 was a big step towards the definitive Beetle shape.

cooled, overhead-valve motor which proved excessively noisy. These problems led to a 12-month extension of the original deadline. Daimler-Benz was brought in to build the bodies and produce detailed cost-analyses of the project.

Three more prototypes were then approved, the first (all designated V3) running in February 1936 and differing externally only in minor details from the V1. Beneath the engine cover, however, was a new 948cc, air-cooled, flat four-cylinder, horizontally-opposed engine, the 'E-Motor'. This was the work of young Austrian engineer, Franz Reimspiess. It was simple, strong and light featuring a cast crankshaft and some advanced alloys in its construction – yet it was cheap to produce in quantity.

The V3 prototypes, plus the re-engined V1 and V2, were tested over 30,000 kilometres (18,750 miles) of hard Alpine driving through the autumn of 1936 and a full engineering report was pre-

pared by the RDA. There were a lot of breakages and the RDA remained sceptical that the car could be produced for the envisaged Reichsmarks 990.

But the People's Car was not to be the preserve of private industry. The Nazi state labour organisation, the Deutsche Arbeits Front (or DAF), took control of the project through a new shell company called Gezuvor (Geschellchaft fur Vorbereitung des Deutschen Volkswagens) with headquarters situated next to Porsche's big new offices. There was more money around now.

In the spring of 1937, a batch of pre-production cars (code-named VW30), were built by Daimler-Benz showing a marked step in evolution towards the eventual Beetle shape. In side profile the body's waistline was higher and the windows smaller. At the front the headlamps were set in fairings in the front wings. From the back there was still no rear window and a central rib was

Main picture: The VW30 prototypes of 1937 featured highly sculptural body styling made even starker by the absence of rear windows and bumpers. Wind tunnel tests registered a coefficient of drag of 0.49. **Above:** A column of VW38s on a selling tour of German cities, late 1938.

pressed into the roofline. Some cars were fitted with bumpers but there no running boards. Mechanically the VW30 featured refinements to the oil-cooler, front suspension and brakes. These cars were each exhaustively tested over 80,000 kilometres (50,000 miles) and in the Adlerhof wind-tunnel. Results were good but there was still a long way to go. Taking breath, Komenda produced his definitive VW body styling, a shape in substance and in detail that remains recognizable more than 50 years later.

The sculptural roof ribbing was bifurcated and moved outwards to near the gutter line. At the rear, a split oval rear window was incorporated, with a single line of louvres now punched into the metal above the hinged engine cover. At the front end the entire boot lid was now made in one piece, hinging upwards at the bulkhead. The characteristic oval headlamps were gracefully faired at an angle into gently bulged front wings. Doors were hinged at the front, hub caps and running boards incorporated.

A batch of 44 of these cars, typenamed VW38, were built and road tested in 1938. Wind tunnel tests showed a drag co-efficient of only 0.385. A further pre-production batch of 50 cars, the VW39 series, was completed by Daimler-Benz by July 1939.

But four years on from Porsche's original contract, the People's Car remained a prototype. There were no dedicated production facilities, no dealerships or after-sales operation in a conventional sense. But planning was in hand, on a grandiose scale. A vast factory would be built on the marshy banks of the Mittelland Kanal at Fallersleben, 50 miles west of Hanover. Target output was 500,000 vehicles a year by 17,500 workers operating in two shifts. These were volumes that only the US giants were achieving.

In 1936-7, Porsche made two trips to the USA. He was able to study American mass-production techniques, negotiate contracts for advanced machine tools, and lure some German-born production engineering specialists back to the Fatherland.

In May 1938, the foundation stone of the new factory was laid in a typically-Nazi ceremony presided over by the Führer himself. The town built to house the workers would be called KdF-Stadt and the car they were to make was renamed the KdF-Wagen, the 'Strength Through Joy' car. Gezuvor meanwhile on 6 October 1938 became Volkswagenwerk GmbH. There would be no conventional dealerships – the KdF-Wagen could only be bought through a saving stamp system, happy German workers merrily pasting five Reichsmarks a month into swastika-bedecked savings-books until they proudly took possession of the Führer's promised wondercar.

(In a bizarre footnote to the KdF story, potential buyers went on sticking up their stamp books throughout the first years of the war. None of them received a car – but after the war a group filed a law suit against VW. In 1961 after years of wrangling they were offered a cash settlement of DM100 or DM600 off the price of a new Volkswagen. Over 80,000 qualified.)

That's how it was depicted in the propaganda anyway. Elaborate brochures were produced. Convoys of prototype cars were run though German cities and KdF-Wagens set up on stands in town squares like the cherry on a cake for the stamp lickers to dream about. By May 1939, some 270,000 Germans had signed up – covering planned production to the end of 1940.

But it was not to be. On 1 September 1939 the Wehrmacht rolled across the Polish frontier. The German people (and the rest of Europe) would be getting guns, not butter – and certainly not Strength Through Joy-mobiles.

CHAPTER TWO

THE BEETLE GOES TO WAR

THE STRENGTH THROUGH JOY CAR WAS ALL SET TO REWARD

THE GERMAN PEOPLE FOR THEIR LABOURS. BUT IN 1939 ADOLF

HITLER HAD OTHER PLANS AND THE BEETLE WENT TO WAR AS

THE KÜBELWAGEN OR 'BUCKET CAR'. IT SERVED WITH GERMAN

FORCES ON EVERY FRONT FROM THE ARCTIC TO THE WESTERN

DESERT, TAKING BEETLE MECHANICS IN EFFECT ON THE MOST

EXHAUSTIVE TEST DRIVE IN HISTORY.

Left: *The front-end of the Type 166* Schwimmwagen, *a wartime amphibious version of the Beetle.* **Above:** *The VW Type 239 was an otherwise standard* Kübel *with a wood burning unit in the nose to feed producer gas to the engine in the rear.*

From the inception of the people's car project, its military potential had been under consideration. German rearmament had proceeded apace from 1935 following a master plan to provide the German army with a range of fighting vehicles including small open utility vehicles, called 'Kübelwagen' or 'bucket vehicles.'

The Porsche Type 60 with its light, strong backbone chassis, and air-cooled engine with no radiator to freeze seemed an ideal platform. The Porsche Büro produced a prototype Kübel in 1938 (the Type 62) based on Type 60 mechanics with a cut down, rounded body and two spare wheels mounted centrally to prevent ditching. A year later a much-more angular-looking body was produced with ribbed panels for reinforcement. By the time the Second World War began on 1 September 1939 a small number of Kübelwagens were in service.

Reports from the field led to detail improvements: the body was reduced in height and the ribbing extended the full height of the

Top and above: The Type 166 *Schwimmwagen* had a sealed waterproof hull, and fold-down outboard propeller with power take-off from the engine. It was fully amphibious but expensive to make and hence went only to elite units in comparatively small numbers.

The standard Type 82 *Kübel* (above is a preserved example in *Afrika Korps* markings owned by a British enthusiast) delivered reliable and rugged mobility to the Wehrmacht in spite of the absence of four-wheel drive. In the snows of Russia its air cooled engine would start in the coldest weather. In the Western desert its low ground pressure kept it plugging through soft sand when heavier vehicles bogged down.

vehicle. A larger, 30-litre, petrol tank was fitted at the front – the spare wheel now being carried on top of the front decking rather than in a recess. Headlamps were moved from the front of the body to the wings. New reduction gears in the rear hubs allowed the civil KdF-Wagen's gearbox to be used without modification while serving military purposes by lowering the overall ratios. Meanwhile ground clearance was raised 3 cm by changing the stub axle position.

This refined vehicle, called the Type 82, went into volume production in February 1940 and was destined to serve on virtually every front. In Russia, the air-cooled motor would start in the most severe cold, while in the Libyan desert, the light, tractable vehicle could be dug out of sand and kept going where heavier four-wheel-drive machines bogged down.

In 1940, work began on an amphibious version of the military VW. It was more intensely engineered machine, with four-wheel-drive, and cost 7.5 times more to make than the original RM 1000 target for the KdF-Wagen. The *Schwimmwagen* featured a water-tight, doorless, hull with a rear-mounted retractable propeller that, when lowered, propelled the machine in still water at 10 kmh (6.2 mph). The Type 128 Model A of 1940 was built in small numbers, followed by the Type 138 Model C in 1941 which featured a backbone chassis. A year later the definitive Type 166 Model C appeared which had a shorter wheelbase, refinements to the

Many variations on the *Kübel* theme appeared under the pressures of war – including the Type 82E, a *Kübel* chassis with KdF saloon bodywork. This one (**above**) has a producer gas unit in the nose. **Main picture:** VW returned to para-military markets post-war with this open-bodied staff-car for police and fire departments built in small numbers in 1949.

The Type 92 *Kommandeurwagen* of 1943, with a three seat KdF body on a strengthened *Kübelwagen* floorpan.

waterproofing and was 40 kg lighter than original Type 128. All models featured a power unit of increased capacity and power, the 985 cc of the Type 82 being increased to 1,131 cc by a simple bore out of the cylinders. The bulk of the 14,382 eventually manufactured went to units of the Waffen-SS. The more powerful engine (with an output of 25 as opposed to 22 hp) was fitted to standard Kübel production from March 1943 onwards.

Meanwhile production of standard KdF-Wagen saloons begun on 15 August 1940, at the height of Hitler's campaign to conquer the west – and continued at a trickle as the tide of war turned. Only 630 were made, most going to Nazi officials and foreign diplomats.

There were more variations of the Beetle on military themes, however – KdF-Wagen bodies using the militarized Kübelwagen chassis and drive train. Small numbers of Type 82E appeared in 1942, the Type 92 Kommandeurwagen in 1943, and the four-wheel-drive Type 87 in the same year.

CHAPTER THREE

WORLDS TO CONQUER

IN 1945 ADVANCING US SOLDIERS FOUND SOME STRANGE

HUMP-BACKED MOTOR CARS IN THE BOMBED OUT RUINS OF

WOLFSBURG. THE BRITISH ARMY ENGINEERS WHO TOOK OVER

THE FACTORY BROUGHT THE VW FAMILY BACK TO LIFE — AND

THE FIRST OF 20 MILLION POST-WAR BEETLES HIT THE ROAD. AN

AUTOMOTIVE LEGEND WAS RE-BORN.

Above: *The ugly duckling of 1945, utterly austere and virtually ignored by the British who took over the factory in 1945.* **Left:** *By 1952, however, the Export Beetle was quite 'luxurious' – with chrome trim and quarter lights and an optional sun-roof.*

On 10 May 1945, a spearhead of the advancing US 102nd Infantry division entered a town near Hanover which did not appear on their maps. It was KdF-Stadt, the model workers' city, dominated by a huge, but near-derelict, factory. Among the rubble they found partly-built aircraft components. In another corner, they found the final assembly line for the Type 82 Kübelwagen – and a few strange-looking, hump-backed passenger cars, along with tooling to make them.

The USAAF had hit KdF-Stadt six times from April 1944 onwards, destroying three quarters of the plant. The four Allies, the US, Great Britain, France and the Soviet Union, divided Germany into zones of occupation, and in the East, anything of industrial use was being shipped to the Soviet Union as reparation.

KdF-Stadt (now renamed Wolfsburg after a nearby castle as an act of de-Nazification) fell into the British zone with a military administration. In July 1945, a detachment of Royal Electrical and Mechanical Engineers personnel took over the plant, and helped restart Kübelwagen production as a way of relieving the British taxpayer of the burden of supporting the Germans.

In August, a British major, Ivan Hirst, took control of the 'Wolfsburg Motor Works'. As a result of his efforts, more than 500 Kübels were built in the summer and autumn of 1945, 700 Type 51s with the KdF body mounted on the Kübel chassis, and nearly 500 vehicles with utility van bodies. A further 58 basic VW saloons (called Type 11 under the new British designation system) were built by the end of the year.

As Volkswagen production increased, Hirst raising an order for 10,000 vehicles from the British Control Commission early in 1946, the political climate was changing. It was evident that West Germany would one day join NATO and that Volkswagen had a future. The British board controlling VW, with Hirst as the executive director, decided to withdraw from day-to-day management. 'We found a chap called Heinz Nordhoff kicking his heels in Hamburg,' said Hirst. 'He had managed Opel's truck plant, but because he had a war honour he couldn't be employed in the US zone. But he was supremely well-qualified and the rules applying in our zone did not prevent him taking a job with us.'

Then, in June 1948, the near-worthless Reichsmark was replaced by the Deutschemark to put German finances on a sound footing. 'It was like flowers in the desert,' said Hirst. 'Everything boomed, and the shops were full of goods now there was real money. Nordhoff was then able to put Volkswagen on its feet.'

Hirst was offered a job by Ford but turned it down 'to see the job out at Volkswagen.' The job at Dagenham was taken by Terence Beckett, father of the Cortina . . . and the former major

Main picture: JLT 420 was built for the British forces in Germany in 1947, imported secondhand to the UK and sold on (duly repainted in a two-tone scheme) by Britain's first VW dealer.

Right: The 'Export engine' in 1947 trim (taken from JLT 420 again).

Far right top: A pre-war portrait of Heinz Nordhoff, General Motors (Opel's) man in Germany. Post war he would steer Volkswagen to worldwide success.

Far right: 1946 and the 10,000th Volkswagen comes down the Wolfsburg production line.

The VW38 cabrio prototype was very much a one-off – it is still owned by the VW company. **Below top:** But in 1948 the bodybuilding firm of Karmann began small scale production of an open Beetle, officially launched on 1 July 1949. Meanwhile factory manager Colonel Charles Radclyffe had a special two-seater built in 1946 (**below centre**) and the firm of Hebmüller built a production two-seater from 1949-53 (**bottom**).

moved on to the industrial side of military security in Germany, then worked with the inter-governmental economic organisation, OECD, in Paris. Today he is still held in honour by Volkswagen's management as the man who saved their firm . . . along with Nordhoff.

The currency reform in the Western zones (although it opened wider the deepening split with the Soviets and engendered the Berlin blockade), laid the foundations for the West German *Wirtschaftswunder:* the 'economic miracle' of the 1950s, in which the Beetle played such a significant part.

The funny little car, scurrying around the western zones of occupation in British Army olive green paint or US Army dark grey, did not yet in 1948 give much of a hint of its automotive conquests to come – but Hirst and Nordhoff saw its potential.

There were others sniffing around, with proposals to ship production wholesale to France or Australia. In February 1948, Henry Ford II went to Wolfsburg to test the car – and to consider outright purchase of the VW operation. The idea was dropped.

In 1945-6 two British engineering reports on the car had been prepared. The second, by Humber engineers, praised the body construction but lambasted the engine as underpowered and noisy – concluding that the unorthodox machine was only of marginal interest. It has been said therefore that the British saved the VW twice – first by keeping the factory going in 1945 and then by leaving Nordhoff alone to pursue the technical and marketing development of the car without interference.

On 6 September 1949, British control at Wolfsburg came to an end and ownership of Volkswagenwerk GmbH was entrusted by

Above: The 1953 Export Model featured chrome horn grilles, quarterlights and the end of the 'split' oval rear window. Under the rear engine cover (**below**) meanwhile there was a new Solex carburettor and redesigned inlet manifold. Engine capacity was increased to 1192 cc from January 1954.

the New German Federal Republic to the State of Lower Saxony. Volkswagen was now German-owned, and Germany's largest single car manufacturer, but there was no room for complacency. Nordhoff took two vital decisions, to concentrate on a single model line (while improving its quality by technical evolution from within) and to attack export markets. The result was the Export model, launched on 1 July 1948, which featured a choice of colour schemes and chrome trim.

A trickle of VWs had been shipped home from Germany by British and US servicemen – but exports proper began through Hirst's support of a former Dutch Opel dealer called Ben Pon who took small numbers in late 1947. In January 1949, Pon shipped a standard grey saloon to New York – to be greeted with deafening indifference by the dealers he tried to get interested in the utilitarian looking vehicle.

Nordhoff tried a year later, armed with pictures of the Export model – and had more luck. One hundred and fifty seven VWs were registered in the US in 1950 – the beginning of an extraordinary marketing success.

Meanwhile, at Wolfsburg, there were more variations on the basic Beetle theme. A four-seater Cabriolet, with a body built by Karmann of Osnabruck, was launched on 1 July 1949. A two-seater roadster, with a special body by the small coachbuilding firm of Hebmüller, had been introduced the month before. Sunshine roofs (a throwback to the KdF 'cabriolimousine' version) became optional from April 1950.

As the decade turned, there was a VW which had **not** been part of Porsche's prewar plans: a commercial derivative, called the

Type 2, or 'Transporter'. There had been several wartime proto-types of van, ambulance and light truck versions of the Type 60, with closed and open bodies grafted somewhat unhappily into the rear-engined Beetle body. Small numbers of utility versions were built after the war. But it was clear to Nordhoff that a new body-shell would be needed to fully utilize the rear-engine layout. Thus the VW Type 2 was born.

The design, by Dr Ing Alfred Haesner, owed little to Porsche and the war years, other than employing the Beetle's running gear and Kübelwagen-type reduction gears at the outer ends of the rear driveshafts. The boxlike body made some styling concessions to its stablemate, however. The rear engine allowed a very clean front-end, with an inverted V pressed into in the rounded prow, echoing the Beetle's front bonnet line. The split window and oval headlamps remained until 1967.

The original batch of Type 2 prototypes, which appeared in November 1949, were based on a standard Beetle backbone-chassis floorpan. But production vehicles, from March 1950, featured a more rugged structure of two box section mainframes running lengthways with five cross members, and the body welded directly on top. The Type 2 was originally offered as a closed van, or 'Kombi', with removable seating, and as an eight-seater bus.

The Type 2 rapidly established itself as a successful stablemate to the Beetle saloon. Production rates in five body styles (in-cluding a flatbed pick-up truck and an ambulance) reached more than 100,000 a year in 1957.

Big changes were made in the Beetle's interior in 1952 which until then had used the original KdF fascia. This right hand drive version (**above**) shows the central grille for the optional radio. **Below:** The completely new body style of the Type 2 Transporter solved the problem of producing a utility vehicle on the Beetle floorplan. Sales began in 1950.

The 1950s was the Beetle's decade. In 1950, the car from Wolfsburg (when the 100,000th Beetle left the factory in March), was a well-engineered and still somehow futuristic oddity hung over from the 1930s. Ten years later it had become an industrial and marketing phenomenon of the first magnitude.

In August 1955 the 1,000,000th Beetle was built, followed by the 3,000,000th in 1959. By 1961, production exceeded 1,000,000 a year, with exports to 136 countries and subsidiary companies in Brazil, America and Australia. In the US it was the top manufactured import in cash terms. New factories were built, at Hanover in 1956, at Kassel in 1958, and at Emden in 1964.

In 1960, 60 per cent of VW's shares were sold to public and institutional investors, the rest being retained by the Federal and State governments. In 1965 Volkswagen GmbH became Volkswagen AG, and in the same year the newly-public company acquired Auto-Union (owned since 1958 by Daimler-Benz) with its main Ingolstadt factory. From the largely dormant Auto-Union product range, the Audi marque was reactivated, offering middle market, conventional, four-cylinder cars while some Beetle production was switched to Ingolstadt.

In August 1969, VW acquired a major shareholding in NSU. One NSU model was grafted into the VW line up, the mid-sized K70 saloon, which lingered on somewhat unhappily under new ownership until 1975.

The Volkswagen company was striving to grow by acquisition as much by growth from within. It was necessary – the glory years of the 1950s and early 1960s (and the days of four Deutschmarks to

Above: The eight-seater VW Micro Bus, one of the very successful variants of the Type 2 'Kombi' transporters.

Below: 6 August 1955; Wolfsburg celebrates the one millionth Beetle to be produced since 1945 – and the VW's golden age was only just beginning!

Above: Interior shot of the 1952 UK Export model. It shows several of the new features, including redesigned fascia, glove compartment and Wolfsburg badge on the steering wheel. **Below and right:** Two views of the 1968 Bug. The continual detail changes advocated by Nordhoff meant the product changed little and bred customer loyalty.

the US dollar which had served to open many American wallets) were ending.

In 1967, VW lost its place as top European car manufacturer to Fiat. The Deutschmark hardened against the dollar. Demand at home and in the vital US market began to falter. The factory went on short time; a company used only to coping with the problems of success seemed to have lost its way. Nordhoff (who was to die in April 1968) was accused bitterly by shareholders, bankers and politicans of having hung on too long to his evolve-one-product-from-within policy.

In reply, he could claim that the VW of 1968 was a complete transformation from the Porsche VW38 prototype of years before. Indeed the very combination of product stability with an approach to engineering of such intellectual rigour that made the announcement of new hub-caps an event of major significance, was the basis of VW's marketing culture and customer loyalty.

Volkswagen GmbH had carried over part of its KdF patrimony in one important respect. The VW was designed by Porsche and his team under contract to a company set up to turn out vehicles in high volume at low unit cost, 'selling' them under state direction to a captive market.

The company proved its brilliance in production engineering,

The 'Notchback' 1500 launched in 1961 (**above**) and the 1600 TL fastback variant launched in 1965 (**below**) were both developed as Beetle replacements as VW entered a decade of uncertainty – but in the 1960s it was the Bug that would triumph again on the sales chart.

quality control and in marketing – but capital investment in pure research and development remained low.

Ferdinand Porsche had returned to Germany in 1947 (after a brief period of capitivity in France) assuming that his first task would be to design a 'modern' replacement for the VW Type 60. His company signed a deal with VW in 1948 to supply its design services (which also gave Porsche a royalty of 5 DM on every Beetle built). But the expected call to radically rejuvenate the Wolfsburg-wonder never came. VW was to rely heavily on the Porsche company's design expertise until 1965 when in-house research facilities (including the building of what was then the motor industry's biggest wind tunnel) were greatly expanded.

Meanwhile the Beetle went through a continuous series of detail fixes and modifications, which left only a single part – the cross section of a metal crease holding a rubber sealing strip on the rim of the engine and luggage compartment covers – unchanged from the beginning of production to the end. (The most important of those changes are chronicled in the next chapter.)

Meanwhile Beetle 'replacements' came and went – the 'notchback' 1500 was launched in 1961 (known as the Type 3), basically featuring Beetle mechanics in a modern-looking three-box body shell. Estate and fastback versions were produced from 1963. The Type 4 Model 411 pushed the principle forward with a rear-mounted 1,679cc flat-four engine in a four-door body, but it achieved nothing like the Beetle's popularity in the US and was dropped from German production in 1974.

This was the Volkswagen company's bleakest year. The oil price hike was shaking the world's economy, and for a company globally geared to consumer demand, the shock of the first loss in the company's history (DM 807m – £142.5m) was total. But the

Above: Dieter Gottlieb and Gunther Janger rallied the Porsche Salzburg-prepared 1600 cc Beetle. It had a specially designed five-speed gearbox.
Below: The German presence in South America – a Brazilian-manufactured Beetle. The later versions were converted to run on alcohol, a petrol substitute made from sugar cane.

investment in new models had come just in time.

In 1973, the Passat, the first of a new generation of front-wheel drive cars, had been launched. In May 1974 something completely new was revealed. It was an economical, efficient and affordable means of moving a family from A to B – the VW Golf. It had a water-cooled engine, front-wheel-drive with a slab-sided body styled by an Italian. A new era in the history of Volkswagen had begun.

CHAPTER FOUR

EVOLUTION FROM WITHIN

VW CHIEF HEINZ NORDHOFF'S DICTUM, TO TAKE THE BEETLE AS

PORSCHE HAD SIRED IT, AND MODIFY ITS BASIC ENGINEERING

YEAR BY YEAR, WAS A GREAT GAMBLE. BUT IN THE DAYS OF

PLANNED OBSOLESCENCE THE VOLKSWAGEN SHONE LIKE A

BEACON OF PRACTICAL GOOD SENSE, EACH CHANGE BEING

CAREFULLY CONSIDERED. AND IN THE LAST DECADE OF ITS

PRODUCTION LIFE, THE PACE OF CHANGE QUICKENED

DRAMATICALLY.

Above: *The beefy rear-end of the 1600 GT Beetle, a more powerful version of the 1600 built in 1973.* **Left:** *An immaculate cabrio registered in 1978 – Karmann ceased production in 1980.*

Throughout its long production life the Beetle was the subject of continual change. Although VW's marketing rationale was based on a haughty aloofness from the vagaries of fashion, the smallest cosmetic change could be greeted with all the attention dedicated by another section of the Press to royal wardrobes. In the 1950s, German motor magazines would dedicate entire features to the revision of a door handle. Some were minor, logical refinements, others were major engineering changes which departed substantially from the Porsche patrimony.

Externally, evolution in body shape and detail was subtle. There are, however, clear breakpoints which mark the ages of the Beetle – the 'split window era,' 1945-53; the 'oval era,' 1953-59, and the late-classic period, 1959-67, leading to the front and rear end styling rework of 1967 with the introduction of recessed vertical headlights. In the 'post classic' period, 1968-1978, the Beetle line spawned the bulbous-bonneted Super Beetle. The 'big' VW also featured a prominent curved windscreen for three years of its production.

Beneath the Volkswagen's skin, there were a myriad of improvements to engine, gearbox, suspension and braking – striving not just for better performance or passenger comfort but for durability and ease of maintenance.

From 1949-65, the Beetle model range was static – featuring the standard saloon, the 'Export' model and the Karmann-bodied cabriolet. There had been special models built on the VW chassis, including the Hebmüller coupes and low-run sporting versions with tuned engines and exotic bodywork by approved non-VW specialist companies in Austria and Switzerland, and, of course, from 1955, the in-house Karmann Ghia. But, after the comparative failure of the Type 3 – the wholesale rebodying exercise of 1961 – the Beetle itself came in for some brand-building as a range of engine capacities and factory options were offered in a

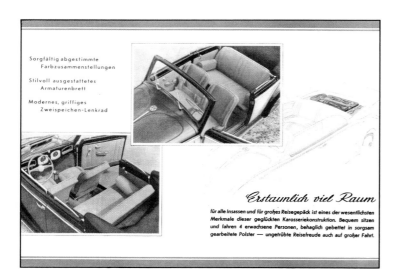

Above: 1950 brochure for the Karmann-built convertible – note the original KdF-pattern fascia. **Main picture:** 'Split' rear window – the early Beetle's most striking identifying feature. The Beetle went oval in 1953. **Far right:** By the early Sixties multiple detail design changes were beginning to show.

The Super Beetle.
We've made so many improvements they're beginning to show.

broadening spectrum of models. And in the late 1960s and early 1970s, the post-Nordhoff management strove mightily to inject some new technology into the Beetle – but these major engineering changes were as much driven by stiffening environmental legislation in the US and in the vital Californian market, as by market whim.

In 1965, the Standard became the 1200 and the Export model the 1200A. The following year the range grew with the 1300 model now offered in tandem, with a 1,285cc engine. In 1967, the 1500 appeared with a 1,493cc engine plus a semi-automatic option from 1968. A substantially re-engineered model, the 1302, was marketed in the US as the 'Super Beetle,' from 1971.

'We've made so many improvements they're beginning to show,' said the Super Beetle's launch publicity in the US – and the vehicle, indeed, remains immediately recognizable as being different. It was 3in (7.5cm) longer than the standard Beetle. Reworking the front suspension with MacPherson struts allowed the luggage are to be enlarged, along with a more bulbous bonnet. The rear suspension was also revised: the swing axle was replaced by double-jointed trailing arms and a new diagonal link.

The 1302/Super Beetle was supplanted by the 1303 in 1973,

Main picture: Two Hebmüller two-seaters owned by a British enthusiast, including an ultra-rare fixed head coupé. **Far left:** An early Seventies Beetle. Its ease of starting in the cold weather was a feature of its advertising in Europe and the U.S. **Above:** US Super Beetle launch publicity reveals the more bulbous front bonnet line accommodating the completely revised McPherson strut front suspension.

which featured a curved windscreen (and hence a shortened bonnet lid) and recessed dashboard, plus restyled rear wings with outsize rear lamp clusters. Options of trim were offered down the range, which continued with the 1200, 1300 and 1600. In 1974, a 'basic 1303' was offered (called the 1303A), with baseline trim and the 1200 engine.

On 1 July 1974, Beetle production at Wolfsburg ended. Manufacture of a shrinking range continued at Emden – the 1303 was dropped in 1975 with the 'flat-windscreen' 1200 run on in 1200L (with a higher trim specification) and 1200S (with the 1600 engine) guises. From 1975, US Beetles were fitted with Bosch electronic fuel injection, restoring some of the horsepower lost to emission control equipment. Production of German-built saloons ended at Emden on 19 January 19 1978. A short reprieve allowed the convertible to survive in the US market – production of 1303/Super Beetle cabrios continuing at Osnabruck until January 1980.

1945-49

The first post-war products from Wolfsburg were KdF-Wagens, austerely trimmed with comparatively crude paintwork and no chrome trim. Flat hubcaps were painted, with the VW monogram stamped in the slightly raised centre. Nordhoff's arrival resulted in the appearance of the Export Model on 1 July 1949 featuring a crop of detail changes:

- Colour range increased
- Chrome trim on headlamps, bonnet and side strips
- Painted horn grills set into front wings
- Bonnet handle fixed, release now by cable from within car
- Chromed, grooved bumpers
- Conical chromed hubcaps featuring VW monogram
- Number plate indentation on engine cover and starting handle deleted
- Adjustable seats with arms rests front and rear
- White facia panels set into dashboard with matching knobs
- Two-spoke white steering wheel

1949 also saw the introduction of the Hebmüller two-seater cabrio and the Karmann four-seater cabriolet.

1950
- Fabric sunroof option offered
- Opening rear ventilation windows as optional extra
- Nick cut in top of front door windows to allow some ventilation control
- Hydraulic brakes on Export model
- Front and rear ashtrays standard on Export model

1951
- Chrome surround to windscreen on Export model
- Wolfsburg badge introduced above boot lid on Export model
- Rear vent windows discontinued replaced by opening flaps in front quarter panels
- Aluminium crankcase replaced by magnesium alloy
- Locking glove box on cabrio

1952
- Pull out vent flaps in quarter panels replaced by opening quarter lights in front windows

- Sixteen inch wheels replaced by 15 in (38 cm)
- New rear number-plate light-housing – single rear stop light-replaced by two-lens rear and stop lights on both wings
- T-handle replaces loop handle on rear engine cover
- Syncromesh added on second, third and fourth gears on Export models
- Redesigned facia, speedometer repositioned immediately in front of driver. Glove compartment gets a cover and a Wolfsburg badge appears on steering wheel
- Interior light moved from rear to nearside door pillar
- Saloon glove compartment gets door
- Wipers self cancelling

1953
- Split rear window replaced by single piece oval rear window (last 'split' window car built 10 March)
- Front torsion bars modified, six leaves increased to eight
- Quarter light windows get lock button
- Handle added to dashboard ashtray

1954
- 1,192 cc engine introduced with detail refinements. Output boosted from 25 bhp to 30 bhp
- Single lens combined stop-rear lamps introduced
- Starter switch combined with ignition key
- Automatic courtesy interior light switches in doors

1955
From 1955 onwards the VW model year started on 1 August.

- Single exhaust pipe replaced by twin chromed pipes on Export cars
- Rear lamps moved upwards around 2 in (5 cm)

1956
- Karmann Ghia introduced. Semi-hand built, Italian-styled coupé body on Export Beetle chassis
- Cranked gear lever, off-centre spokes to steering wheel, three position front seat adjustment

The 1960 VW floorpan. Front suspension king pins lasted until 1965 when they were replaced by ball joints. Front disc brakes replaced drums on the 1500 in 1967.

1957
- Semaphore indicators replaced by podded flashers on front wings of US cars
- Improved engine sound proofing
- Engine cover louvres changed from vertical to horizontal on cabrio

1958
- Windscreen enlarged
- Larger rear window (last 'oval' window car built 31 July)
- Engine cover remodelled, flare below number plate light cut back
- Revised facia with vertical rather than horizontal slats
- Roller accelerator pedal replaced by treadle type

1959
- Angle of forward tilt of engine and gearbox increased by 2 degrees
- Karmann Ghia convertible introduced
- Horizontal air inlets replace vertical louvres on engine cover of Karmann cabrio
- Pod front indicators moved to top of wings on US models

1960
- Push button door handles
- Semaphores replaced by front wing flashers and indicators in rear lamp clusters on European models
- Dished steering wheel with horn ring
- Padded sun visor replaces transparent green plastic

1961
- Redesign of petrol tank affords a 65 per cent increase in usable luggage space
- Detail improvements to engine: compression ratio raised to 7:1 with top speed increased from 68 to 72 mph (109-115 kph). Automatic choke
- Syncromesh on bottom gear

- Worm and roller steering replaces worm and nut
- Sun visor and grab handle on passenger side
- Pump action windscreen washer

1962
- Larger three-piece rear light clusters
- Dashboard fuel gauge fitted
- Front bonnet spring loaded

1963
- Wolfsburg crest bonnet badge discontinued
- Nylon window guides
- Leatherette headliner

Top: The 1962 model year 1200.

Above: A '61 cabrio.

Both featured sizeable engineering changes under the skin.

VW BEETLE: A CELEBRATION

Above: '64 US-spec Bug. Bumper overrider bars featured on US cars from 1956. **Below:** Rear suspension, engine and gearbox on the '67 model. 'Softer' torsion bars reducing roll stiffness answered some old criticism of the VW's handling characteristics.

1964

- Factory fitted crank operated steel sunroof option replaces canvas/PVC fabric
- Wider rear number plate light
- Aerated PVC seat covers
- Spoke mounted thumb operated horn knobs
- Larger rear number plate light housing

1965

- Standard model designated 1200
- Major body changes – windows enlarged, slimmer door and windscreen pillars
- Push button catch on engine cover
- Rear-seat folds down flat
- Front suspension layout modified – kingpin and stub axle layout supplanted by new ball-joint system plus new shock absorbers
- Heater control levers mounted on tunnel

1966

- 1300 model introduced with 1,285cc, 50 bhp engine. Features ventilated wheels with flattened hub caps, combined indicator/flasher stalk, emergency flasher switch

1967

- 1500 model introduced with 1,493cc, 53 bhp engine. Features redesigned engine cover with central rib deleted and square cut bottom, and revised rear suspension with softer torsion bars
- 1300 model features revised engine cover

Above: 1978 1200 cc Beetle, showing the relocation of the indicators to the front bumpers, first incorporated in 1975. **Below:** *The Love Bug* was film about VW Bug with a mind of its own. Several 'Herbie' production specials were produced to satisfy people's demands for their own Herbie.

- US cars feature vertically mounted headlights
- 12 volt electrics on US cars
- Ventilating slots in wheels and flat hub caps
- Front disc brakes on 1500 model
- Dual circuit braking on US vehicles

1968
- European vehicles feature US-style vertical headlights
- 12-volt electrics on European vehicles
- External fuel filler cap under spring loaded cover on front right quarter panel
- Fresh air ventilation sytem introduced on 1300/1500. Louvres punched in bulkhead in front of windscreen
- Big wrap round bumpers on 1300/1500
- Semi automatic gearbox option on 1500
- Flattened door handles with locking buttons
- Dual circuit breaking on European vehicles
- Collapsible steering column
- Rear swing axles deleted and now exposed drive shafts fitted with universal joints at each end. New diagonal link gives semi-trailing arm geometry
- Emission control equipment on US vehicles
- Head restraints on front seats

1969
- Semi automatic gearbox option on 1300
- Hot rear window
- Combined steering lock/ignition switch
- Front bonnet release from inside vehicle

Above: This UK specification 1968 1500 shows the new pattern lamp clusters and big wrap-round bumpers – plus a further increase in rear window area.
Below: A 1600 cc Super Beetle. The Super Beetles were first introduced in 1970 and featured a number of changes.

1970

- 1302 model introduced (Super Beetle in US) featuring Mac-Pherson strut front suspension, revised rear suspension, new boot layout, ventilation outlets at back of rear windows, bulbous bonnet with squared-off front end
- 1500 features extra louvres in engine cover
- Enlarged front indicators incorporating side repeaters on US vehicles, side reflectors on rear lamp clusters

1971

- 1302S model introduced in Europe with 1,584cc engine featuring a stronger crankcase, new twin inlet-port cylinder heads and redesigned manifolding
- two-speed wipers
- four-spoke padded centre steering wheel

Left: The 1302 featured major chassis and body changes.
Below: The 1971 model year 1300 replaced the 1500 which was discontinued.

VW Beetle Convertible.

The Seventies may be light-years away from the Fifties, but as one generation after another has discovered, there's something unique and timeless about the sheer fun and exhilaration of driving our Beetle Convertible. And today, after 28 years, umpteen million Beetles and countless changes, we're proud to report that the 1978 is one of the best Convertibles we've ever built.

Even though it's one of the least expensive convertibles you can buy.

In fact, our Beetle Convertible is quite unlike anything else you can buy.

Starting at the top, you'll find top quality vinyl that's windproof, waterproof and easy to clean. Inside, it's fully insulated and upholstered. Even the metal braces are covered. And in back, there's a rear window that's a real window. Made of glass, and electrically heated to keep off snow and ice.

For your comfort, there are adjustable headrests and well-padded, stylish leatherette seats. And for great performance and economy, there's our reliable 1.6 liter engine with fuel injection. According to EPA estimates*, our Beetle Convertible delivers 30 mpg highway, 21 mpg city.

As you can see, when we promise you the sun, the moon and the stars, we go to great lengths to deliver.

*Based on 1978 EPA estimated mileage with manual transmission. Your actual mileage may vary, depending on where and how you drive, your car's condition and optional equipment. Ask your local dealer for a free copy of the EPA/FEA Gas Mileage Guide for New Car Buyers.

THE SUN, THE MOON AND THE STARS ARE YOURS TO ENJOY.

CONTROL 8 FUNCTIONS FROM THE STEERING COLUMN.

LUXURIOUSLY UPHOLSTERED, SPACIOUS SEATING.

THE ONLY SMALL FOUR-PASSENGER CONVERTIBLE IN PRODUCTION TODAY.

Above: US publicity for the 1977 cabrio. The open car was based on the Super Beetle specification right to the end of production in 1980. **Main picture:** Wolfsburg celebrates the moment when the Beetle overtook the Ford Model T in 1974 as the world production record car.

Above: 1972 saw the arrival of the 1303 with a radically revised, rounded windscreen.

1972

- 1303 model introduced featuring rounded windscreen and shorter bonnet lid, bigger wrap round bumpers, outsize rear lamp clusters, completely redesigned facia in non-reflective black with rocker switches, fresh air venting and a hooded speedometer
- Built-in diagnostic connector added

1973

- Multi-position front seat adjustment
- Inertia-reel safety-belts

1974

- 1200 gets wrap round bumpers
- Self-restoring energy absorbing bumpers on US models
- Seat belt ignition cut out interlock on US vehicles

1975

- Big rear lamp clusters fitted across range
- Indicator flashers relocated from top of wings to front bumpers
- Fuel injection on US vehicles
- California models with catalytic converter require unleaded petrol
- Lower clutch pedal-pressure
- Rack-and-pinion steering replaces worm and roller on 1303

1976

- Model range shrinks to 1200 (with Super Beetle Cabriolet in small scale production). The 1200 continues with 'traditional' mechanics: front torsion bars, swing-axle rear suspension plus worm-and-roller steering

1977

- Adjustable headrests replace integrated headrests
- Plush velour upholstery

1978

- German production of saloons ends

1980

- Production of cabrio ends in January at Karmann

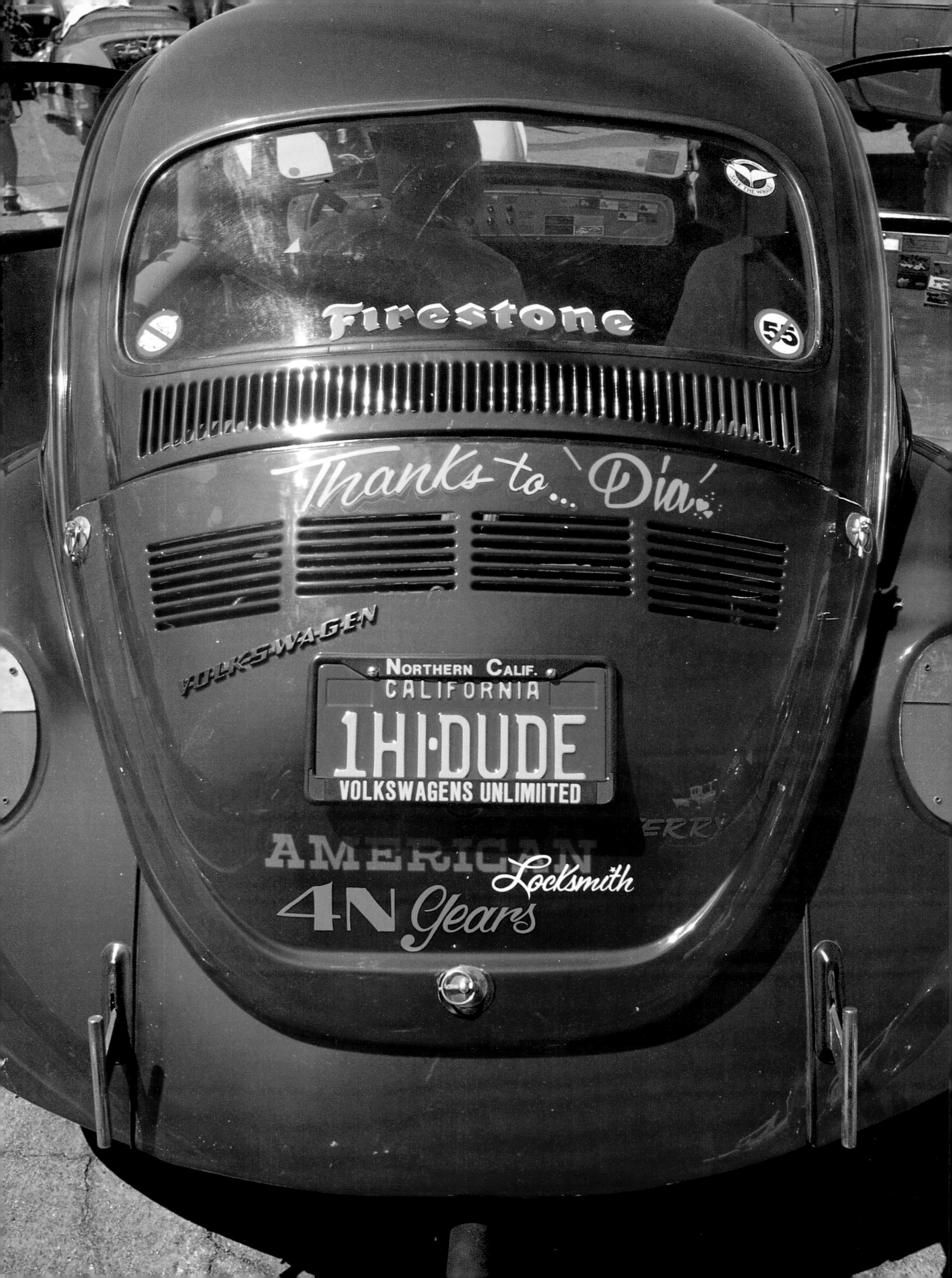
Firestone
55
Thanks to... Dia
VOLKSWAGEN
NORTHERN CALIF.
CALIFORNIA
1HI·DUDE
VOLKSWAGENS UNLIMIITED
AMERICAN
Locksmith
4N Gears

CHAPTER FIVE

THE BEETLE IN THE U.S.

WHEN THE FIRST VWS WERE SHIPPED TO NEW YORK IN 1949,

THE STRANGE-LOOKING CAR FROM WOLFSBURG BOMBED. BUT

VW KEPT TRYING AND IN 1955 SET UP VW OF AMERICA, THE

BEGINNING OF A SALES PHENOMENON UNIQUE IN

AUTOMOTIVE HISTORY — AS 1960S AMERICA BECAME GRIPPED

BY VW-FEVER.

Some Americans take the Bug (as they call the Beetle) very seriously indeed – others have been known to do the most outrageous things to their Bug.

'Why Do So Many People Buy Volkswagens?' asked the 1968 US bug publicity. 'In our first year we sold two cars – since then we've sold 2,000,000. The marketing men of Volkswagen of America knew the answer, of course, and just then, when demand far outstripped supply, they didn't have to bother with a hard sell.

'Sixty eight was the year of the Bug. In 12 triumphant months, 390,379 saloons were sold in the American market, plus 9,595 convertibles and 50,756 Type 2 Transporters, the best year ever for VWoA,' they trumpeted. The ugle bug from Wolfsburg had scuttled its way to the heart of American consumer-culture.

There was no magic formula. By now the VW enjoyed no cheap labour cost or exchange-rate pricing advantage (the Deutschmark was ever hardening against the US dollar). Why so many Americans were buying Volkswagens by the late 1960s was the re-sult of hard work by a brilliant marketing team – building on very small beginnings, in a story that mirrored the rebirth of the Wolfsburg wonder itself.

The United States emerged from the Second World War as a military and industrial superpower. War was good for the US economy – the Korean War triggered a period of unparalleled growth in the 1950s. In the 1960s, too, the Vietnam conflict was good for an economy in which 'conspicuous consumption' ruled. Ironically the Beetle prospered by symbolising the very opposite.

The boom of the Eisenhower years was reflected *par excellence* in the offerings of Detroit at the time, when a model year meant just that and 'planned obsolescence' dominated – and when US auto-manufacturers were at the very height of their F-86 fins and nosecone styling obsession, churning out gas-guzzling monsters. The very baroqueness of these turnpike-cruising Wurlitzers gave

Above: Puzzled US pump attendant meets a '57 Bug. Humour played a big part in the VW's journey to the heart of US autoculture, whether in New York or (**right**) in the New Mexico desert.

VWoA a marketing gambit which they seized brilliantly. The dictate to the advertisers was to keep the message downbeat: the Volkswagen was cool, practical and rational, a car for the intelligent, a proto-mammal scampering round the scaly feet of the Detroit dinosaurs.

It nearly did not happen at all. In 1949, Pon arrived in New York with a single car in an attempt to enlist dealers. None were interested. The next year Nordhoff himself arrived to conclude a deal with a specialist importer of luxury cars, the Austrian Max Hoffman. He managed to shift only 3,000 in three years and in late 1953 Hoffman was quietly dropped. For a third attempt, two company salesmen (one of whom couldn't speak English) were sent to the US to set up a fledgling marketing operation with a base on the East and West coasts. It began to work. A national dealership chain with an exceptionally diligent parts and service operation began to grow.

On April 15 1955, Volkswagen of America was formed with headquarters in New York (moving to New Jersey in 1962). An ambitious plan to set up a US-production line in the defunct Studebaker factory was however shelved. Sales grew steadily, 47,446 in 1957, 52,221 in 1958, 84,677 in 1959, not setting the world on fire, but winning a place in the affection of an *influential* group of Americans.

From Greenwich Village to San Francisco, a liberal establishment of academics, writers, actors and the like adopted the car as a symbol of resistance to the energy-gobbling affluence around them. Its Nazi origins were forgotten, its Teutonic efficiency expounded.

When Carl Hahn, formerly a bright young economist in the Wolfsburg export department, arrived in New Jersey in 1959 to take over VWoA, his first task was to push outwards from this loyal, but small, constituency. He aimed to sell a VW to a mid-West storekeeper's wife, not just a Hollywood art director. He was shrewd enough to appoint Doyle Dane Bernbach as VWoA's new advertising agency – and they were bright enough to see just how powerful an image they had to build upon in the 'intelligent' choice of automobile.

'Think small,' said the pilot ads, extolling the virtues of a well-engineered, easy-to-maintain, fuel-efficient package. 'How does the man who drives the snowplow get to the snowplow,' they asked – with an answer expanding upon the cold-start abilities of the VW's air-cooled engine. 'It's ugly, but it gets you there,' was the line run under a picture of Apollo's lunar excursion module the day after the 1969 moon landing. In the 1960s VW advertising in the US set a standard of brilliant understatement which won creative awards at the same rate as it won VW buyers. Annual

Late Sixties advertising for the Beetle in the United States emphasised the car's size (**above left and centre**) and its appeal to the youth market, like the surfing fraternity on the West Coast (**above right**).

Left: Local dealers were also involved in interesting advertising gimmicks – Gus Mozart created a 'push-me-pull-you' Beetle.

The customizing of VW Bugs started as a West Coast phenomenon and spread through the US to Europe and the rest of the world. **Preceding pages:** A VW panel van, with highly individual graphics. **Above:** Retro styling reminiscent of a '38 Lincoln Zephyr Coupe.

sales passed the 100,000 mark in 1960, 200,000 in 1963, and 300,000 in 1967.

But wit couldn't cloak the fact that the Beetle had growing competition. The spurt of VW's success in the late 1950s had led to Detroit's 'compact' fight back of 1960 with a range of down-sized automobiles from GM and Ford. The rush of Detroit 'wimpmobiles' did not dent VW's sales performance at all, although it did cut into other European and notably British small car imports. In the 1950s the Morris Minor had pegged VW sales as a quaint

European import. By the 1960s, it was nowhere.

But by 1970, there were new challenges for the German car. The Japanese manufacturers were on the march. The Deutschmark was much harder against the dollar, pushing up retail price and squeezing profit margins. And US legislators, particularly in California, were setting Wolfsburg engineers increasing problems keeping the Beetle abreast with safety and emission regulations.

Key changes in the Beetle specification were driven by such requirements. Semi-automatic transmission, vertically-mounted

headlamps, dual-cirlcuit breaking, 12-volt electrics, collapsible steering column, revised indicator equipment, front-seat head restraints – were all detail changes led by the American market through the late 1960s.

The 'Super Beetle' of 1971 incorporated all these improvements and fixes in a stretched and substantially re-engineered machine aimed squarely at the US. In 1973, the Super Beetle featured a big curved windscreen, a state-of-the-art matt black plastic facia and a host of creature comforts, warning lights, buzzers and safety

Above left: VW Bug meets Winnebago in this unusual camper conversion. **Above right**: The beach buggy craze of the Sixties – inspired by the Meyers Manx, the first limited production off-road Beetle – enters middle age. **Opposite top**: VW trike on Daytona Beach. **Below**: VW hot rod, with its 460-cu in V8 Chevy engine producing 600 bhp.

equipment. But unlike some of the competition, the Beetle could not soak up extra weight and power-damping emission control equipment without performance suffering noticeably. In the wake of the 1973 oil price hike, the Beetle was also looking thirsty (26 mpg on urban cycle) compared with the newer technology imports. Electronic fuel injection was introduced in 1973 and Beetles sold in California, fitted with catalytic converters, were configured to run on unleaded petrol.

But however 'green' the Beetle claimed to be, the number of fixes the small, intensely engineered package could soak up was limited. The Super Beetle was dropped from the US market in 1976 after a wave of special editions including such baroque confections as 'The Sun Bug' and 'La Grande Bug.' This last over-the-top marketing whim featured corduroy seat inserts, rosewood appliqué on the facia and gearbox console, thick pile carpet and metallic paintwork in 'Lime Green' or 'Ancona Blue' . . .

Dressing up the Beetle as Detroit-iron was a last gasp. The 'classic' Volkswagen (the standard 1200 in effect) was cunningly reintroduced to America and was run on for another year as sales for 1977 dwindled to a mere 12,090.

The idea of 'Special editions' might have made Nordhoff turn in his grave – but from the earliest days there had been a special choice of Beetle which Americans, and particularly those who

Left: Baja Bug bred for off-road racing – lightweight bodywork on a specially-developed frame. **Above:** Centres dealing specifically with restoration as well as customizing have been on the increase in the US.

basked in the warmth (and smog) of Southern California took to their hearts – this was the Beetle convertible.

California Dreaming – The Karmann Cabriolet

An open Beetle had been part of the plans for the KdF-Wagen. Hitler had driven in a one-off prototype at the 1938 foundation-stone ceremony – but there had been no series production. In 1946, the old-established Osnabrook coachbuilding firm of Karmann, itself emerging from the ravages of war, began to discuss

A modern customised VW Beetle cabrio (**above**). Few changes have been made to the original classic, flowing lines of the convertible Bug's shape, as can be seen in this 1959 catalogue (**below**). Modern aerodynamic styling makes the Beetle look just as fresh a design today as it did when it first appeared.

with VW the prospect of producing a special-bodied open version of the car, continuing a particularly German tradition of producing 'cabriolet' soft-tops. Nordhoff approved the plan, but it was not as simple as cutting the steel lid off a Beetle and replacing it with some metal hoops and yards of flapping canvas. The Beetle itself did not have a fully unitary construction body, but nor did it have the girder chassis of its 1930s contemporaries.

Strengthening side girders had to be engineered into the floor-pan to replace the body integrity lost without a stiffening steel roof, while the windscreen top was flattened to take the hood – which folded back into a massive package at the rear, typical of

Left: Humbug awaits the start of a run at the Santa Pod raceway, in Great Britain.
Above: Drag racing at Raceway Park, Baylands in California. Raising the front wheels doesn't mean that Speed ProEnt is going any faster than its opponent but it does look spectacular.

pre-war German luxury tourers. But however pram-like in looks this marriage of 1930s moderne and old-style coachbuilding turned out, the Karmann cabrio had a unique style and feel that was to last, unchanged in essence for more than 30 years. It stayed in production while everywhere else the convertible car fell from grace – and then rose again as a marketing concept. Ironically the car that spearheaded the rag-top comeback in the late 1970s was the car that supplanted the open Beetle at Osnabruck, the VW Golf cabrio.

The Beetle cabrio was based on the Export model chassis, introduced alongside it on July 1, 1949. Costing more than half as much again as the standard saloon, the cabrio received the styling updates and increases in engine capacity of its Wolfsburg cousin, as, if not before, they were introduced into standard production.

The launch of the 1300 and 1500 models in 1967-68 carried into the cabrio line, as did the styling rework of 1968. From August 1970 the open car was based on the big Super Beetle with MacPherson strut front-suspension and a more bulbous prow. In 1973, cabrio versions of the 1303 and 1303S were launched featuring either 1300cc or 1600cc engines and the new capaciously curved windscreen, which incidentally led to a redesign of the hood.

But the Beetle was not immortal, nor was the rag-top. Its primary market in the mid 1970s was the US where the consumer-backlash against pollution was also condemning rag-tops as 'unsafe.' It was also getting expensive ($6179 in 1979), and sales were spinning down from 12,000 in 1971 to 3500 in 1976.

When production of the 1303 and 1303S Beetle saloons ended at Wolfsburg, it seemed that the cabrio must die with it. But a

reprieve was granted as enough Americans demanded the car, run on as an open version of the 1303, to make continued production just about viable. Diane Keaton drove one in Woody Allen's film *Annie Hall* – typical of a new 'preppy' market who saw the cabrio as an essential fashion accessory.

Under sentence of death, cabrio sales actually climbed back to 10,681 units in the USA in 1979. In the last year of official VWoA sales, 1980, the figure was 4572, a few of the last-built being put into mothballs by ardent VW-lovers.

The American love affair with the Beetle was a romance as torrid that anything Hollywood could have dreamed up. It began with rejection of the cool, ungainly European. Then in the late 1950s, the VW batted its oval-eyelids once more and the Americans began to fall. By 1968, the American nation was head

A tastefully upgraded cabriolet. The soft-top Beetle became very popular on the West Coast in the Sixties and remained desirable, ensuring that the cabrio outlasted its 'saloon' brother, selling well in the States up to 1980.

over heels in love.

The love affair continues. With the last German-built Beetles long out of production, VW owners clubs and VW worship continue to prosper and proliferate with enthusiast collectors eschewing a garage full of Duesenbergs for the thrill of driving an original 'split' at 55 mph. Old bug-eyes is back.

CHAPTER SIX

DESIGNER HEAVEN

WHEN IN 1955, VW SOUGHT A WAY OF ADDING SOMETHING

SPECIAL TO THE RANGE, THEY TURNED TO AN ITALIAN STYLING

HOUSE TO COME UP WITH A 'SPORTING' CAR BASED ON THE

VW FLOORPAN. GHIA DESIGNED IT, THE KARMANN COMPANY

BUILT THE BODIES — THE RESULT IS ONE OF THE TWENTIETH

CENTURY'S DESIGN CLASSICS.

Above: *Head turning chic, the Karmann Ghia is even more fashionable today than when it was first launched.* **Left:** *This 1970 version of the Karmann Ghia incorporated new front flashers and larger rear lamp clusters.*

For automotive style fanciers, the Karmann Ghia 'sporting' Volkswagen is still one of the most desirable of auto-arte-facts – three and a half decades after its sinuous body shape first appeared on a Turin drawing board, a design classic as enduring as a Braun calculator or Magistretti chair.

The car blended Germanic engineering thoroughness and Italian high style, extraordinary not just in its aesthetic purity but by the fact that such a flamboyant confection should have come from Volkswagen at all, a company committed at the time of the Karmann's Ghia's inception to ruthlessly extracting maximum profit and production-engineering efficiency from the Beetle and the Beetle alone.

By the mid 1950s, after 1,000,000 Beetles had rolled down the Wolfsburg production line in 10 years, the single product dictum still had plenty of mileage, But, the marketing men at Wolfsburg at least were arguing the case for something a little different to stimulate sales at home and contribute to the great forthcoming assault on the United States.

The bright young men of the newly-established VW of America, in San Francisco and New Jersey, had proved they could certainly shift Bugs, but they too were clamouring for some light and shade in the product range.

Remember too how different the VW design philosophy was from that of Detroit at the time, when a model year meant just that and 'planned obsolescence' ruled.

We have seen how that message of simplicity and reliability worked for the Bug. But could it be used at another end of the market? What about a stylish 'sporting' car which would claim the VW's engineering reputation as its own from its very launch. As VWoA once proclaimed in its advertising, here was 'A Volkswagen for people who can't stand the sight of a Volkswagen.'

And so the Karmann Ghia was born – 'Karmann' for the long-established firm of Osnabrook coachbuilders and 'Ghia' for the Turin-based Carrozzeria Ghia, where Luigi Serge would design the bodywork. It would be stylish and sporting, pitched in price above the top-of-the-range Beetle but well below the exclusive Beetle-bodied Porsche 356.

The Karmann Ghia's chassis was straight Export Beetle, slightly widened and reinforced where necessary, with the current 1,192cc engine at the rear, and slight modifications to the carburettor and oil bath filter. Wrapped around the Beetle mechanics was a coachbuilt body of striking elegance – a shape which owed something to Porsche and Komenda's original curvaceous *Strom-linien* but little else.

The 'KG' coupe appeared in October 1955 and its flying saucer looks immediately grabbed attention. This was not a body designed for mass production from a minimum of stampings. Its smooth and slippery lines looked all of a piece but in fact the body was a sinuous amalgam of compound curves. The pertly jutting nose, for example, was fabricated from three separate panels,

Above: Karmann already had a long-established connection with VW through the production of the convertible version of the Beetle. The link was strengthened with the Ghia-designed 'sporting' Volkswagen.

Right: Early production at Karmann's Osnabruck factory where much of the KG's body was virtually hand built. Note the original front end-treatment with low headlamp line and two-slat 'nostrils'.

Above: A superb '57 KG coupé owned by a US-enthusiast. **Left:** A group of Karmann enthusiasts get together for a rally in Britain. The front one even has half a KG as a trailer.

although there was not a seam to be seen and the level of finish of these virtually hand-built cars was high.

Beneath this elegant skin there were further detail differences to the Beetle. The Karmann Ghia's seats were lower, thus the rake of the steering was at a different angle and required a redesigned drop arm. The dashboard was restyled, although the steering wheel was the same. In front of the driver were two instruments, a large speedometer on the left and a matching electric clock on the right. Ventilation was improved with controls from the dashboard fed by intakes in the nose.

Those small frontal 'nostrils' are an important part of the Karmann Ghia's overall look. Originally, they were simple oval openings cut across by two plain slats. In 1959 the intakes were enlarged and closed off with a three-slat grille, while the front wings were redesigned to raise the headlamps by a few centimetres, in

line with US regulations. The front end of these pre-1960 cars is therefore subtly different to that of later production models and arguments among KG-cognoscenti are equally subtle over which front-end is the more pleasing.

Everyone agrees, however, over the prettiness and desirability of the convertible version (first introduced in September 1957 in left-hand-drive form and designated Type 141). The convertible's front end was reworked along with the coupe in the facelift of 1959 and both coupe and open cars had further minor modification to the interior, while mechanically keeping pace with the Beetle, over subsequent production years. In 1961, came the 43 bhp engine with all-synchromesh gearbox. A 1300 engine was offered in 1966, replaced a year later by the 1500 – with a semi-automatic gearbox on offer from 1968. In 1970, the body was modified to incorporate new front flashers and larger rear lamp clusters in-

Above: A Karmann Ghia Type 3 'razor edge', strictly for the European market. **Top:** One of a kind, the prototype Type 3 KG convertible.

corporating reversing lamps.

Production for the home market ceased in 1973 while the KG's still-lingering appeal in the USA kept exports rolling until June 1974, when the model was finally discontinued. Total production figures were 364,401 coupes and 80,899 convertibles.

Low volume production, and the large degree of hand work which went into the Osnabruck built cars, allowed VW to introduce a further variation on the 'sporting' VW theme, this time based on the VW Type 3 1500 (the 'Notchback') introduced in early 1961.

In 1962 a Karmann Ghia version appeared, which followed the sports coupe formula of the Beetle-based KG, but with a much more technocratic razor-edged body styled by Sergio Sartorelli. This had an aggressive eyebrow ridge over the headlamp clusters, which continued down the body sides to terminate in clipped, and

angular, rear-end treatment. There was no production conve[rtible] tible version because of body stiffening problems, although a p[ro]totype was produced in 1962 and a convertible was feature[d in] marketing literature.

But the Type 3 'razor-edge' Karmann Ghia was not a com[mer]cial success and there were no official American exports, alth[ough] some were shipped individually to Southern California [at the] height of VW-fever in the mid-1960s. Production ceased [] after 42,498 had been manufactured.

INDEX